SEVENOAKS, RIVERHEAD AND SEAL

IN OLD PHOTOS AND POSTCARDS

MATTHEW BALL

First published in Great Britain in 2024
by Matthew Ball

A CIP catalogue record for this book is available
from the British Library.

ISBN: 978-1-3999-6482-1

Cover and layout design by Chandler Book Design
www.chandlerbookdesign.com

Printed in Great Britain by
Short Run Press Limited

For Steph Harrison
and
my beloved aunt
Valerie Ann Davies

PRODESSE QUAM CONSPICI

Peter Nouaille,
Greatness.

A bookplate from the Library of Peter Nouaille III, owner of a silk mill at Greatness. He died in 1809, and was buried at Christ Church, Spitalfields, where his great grandfather had first arrived from France.

The Latin translates as 'to be of service rather than to be conspicuous'.

CONTENTS

Introduction   1

Acknowledgements   3

1. Public Houses   7

2. Hotels   21

3. War   27

4. Transport   37

5. Leisure and Celebrations   49

6. Knole   57

7. Tubs Hill and Station Parade   67

8. London Road   73

9. Upper High Street   83

10. High Street   95

11. Kippington   107

12. The Vine   113

13. St John's   121

14. Riverhead   143

15. Seal   153

Image Credits   162

Bibliography   163

About the Author   165

INTRODUCTION

This is my third book on the town of Sevenoaks. The first two focused on the Great War and the period immediately after. Searching for suitable illustrations for those prompted my interest in collecting local postcards and old photographs.

Having always used social media to help with my research, the arrival of Covid 19 prompted me to create a Facebook page focused on the Second World War when, during 2020, we were unable to proceed with planned public commemorations for the 75th anniversary of the end of the conflict. The popularity of this page led me to rename and continue it as Sevenoaks History Hub. This page has become a place for me to share images from Sevenoaks past, but also for followers to share their own family photos and memories. The page has also become a forum for people to reconnect, exchange long forgotten memories, and seek help for new research projects themselves.

A book seems like a natural progression to these initiatives and I have tried to fill it with images that have not been used previously in similar books. In that, I have been helped by Brian Eveleigh, a fellow collector for whom this has been a much longer passion. Brian has generously shared several images that enhance this book, and I am grateful to him. I also owe thanks to Keith Wade, for sharing his deep knowledge of the history of the pubs and inns of Sevenoaks and allowing the use of images from his collection.

All aspects of life feature in this volume. From the great houses of the town to the more humble workers cottages of St John's, and everything in between, from much missed pubs, to life 'below stairs' at Knole.

There are a number of books that look at the local and social history of Sevenoaks and any new author is indebted to these and to chroniclers of Sevenoaks past, such as Bob Ogley, and the late Gordon Anckorn. I hope that this book will find its place amongst theirs. The images in this volume speak for themselves but I have also included some memories from Sevenoaks residents, past and present, whose recollections add colour to the pictures they accompany.

The town has changed considerably over the years and some lost landmarks are still lamented, like The Farmers, and the original Bligh's bus station. I hope that this book captures a flavour of the past in a way that resonates with readers and encourages us to preserve what we have. The public realm is ours. Historians have a duty to remember. As citizens, we have a responsibility to call for good planning and design, to ensure that no more of value is lost, and what we have is preserved in a town that still has so much to celebrate.

I hope you enjoy this book and that it prompts some happy memories.

Matthew Ball
St John's, Sevenoaks, 2023

7oakspostcardbook@gmail.com
sevenoakshistoryhub.org

ACKNOWLEDGEMENTS

My thanks to everyone who has been kind enough to share some of their own family photos and memories.

Thank you to John Chandler of Chandler Book Design for bringing my vision for this book to life in such a creative way.

I am grateful to Sevenoaks Town Council for their contribution toward the production of this book.

Thanks to Ian Walker for reading this book and for his valuable comments. Thanks also to his wife, Sue, and son, Miles, if only because Miles Walker should definitely see his name in a book for the energy and enthusiasm with which he approaches sport, history, and life.

Steph Harrison has been a friend and a tireless supporter of my work as well as a champion of Sevenoaks and its community. Steph is also an inspirational fundraiser for the charity, Breast Cancer Awareness. It is a great privilege to dedicate this book to her.

Simon Barber has not only reinvigorated Sevenoaks library's public engagement with local history on social media but been a generous and helpful guide to its picture archive. My thanks to him and Liz Botterill of Sevenoaks Museum.

The Sevenoaks Society has been a valuable source of information through their publications, articles and exhibitions.

Thanks to Pauline and Andy Smith for their early interest in the potential for a book like this, and for their long friendship.

I am always grateful to Mum and Dad for all their support, each day they prove that they're the best parents you could wish for. Thanks also to my wider family, including my cousins Peter and Patti Rowley, whose company and stories enrich life every time I see them.

Thank you to those who proofread this book and made a number of helpful comments and suggestions: Tim Sanderson, Ian Walker, and Angela Prior-Wandesforde. They helped make this a better book, but any errors or omissions are mine alone.

Finally, my thanks to Wealden Properties, a business built up over many years by Mr William Terry (known to most as Bill) with a focus on the St Johns Hill, Holly Bush Lane and Dartford Road areas of Sevenoaks. Many of the properties that feature in this book were acquired and developed by Bill, and he was a popular and well-known figure in the community. Bill passed away in August 2023 at the age of eighty-nine, and I am pleased that Wealden Properties has sponsored this book in his memory.

*Detail from a map published in 1870, showing many of
the places referred to in this book.*

I

PUBLIC HOUSES

The story of the pubs of Sevenoaks replicates the national trend of closure and decline. Many once thriving local houses have been converted for other use, from domestic to restaurants and offices. The St John's and Hartslands area that could once boast of ten public houses is now reduced to just one, The Rifleman on Camden Road. Pubs were an important focal point within their communities, publicans were well-known, as were regulars and their 'usual'. Fortunately, many of the buildings survive, standing as a reminder of their former glory.

A mid-Victorian view of the High Street, showing the old Bethlehem Farmhouse, later named Bligh's Hotel. The Parris tea rooms can be seen opposite.

The Holmesdale Tavern, which could boast of five bars, stood in the High Street in one incarnation or other since at least 1860. This photo was taken during The Great War, with two soldiers belonging to a transport section posing outside. The pub was supplied by the nearby Holmesdale Brewery owned by John Bligh. By the time of this photo, Bligh had sold the brewery to Watney Combe Reid.

The Royal Oak stands at the top of Oak Lane. The nearest cottage in the row of four opposite was demolished in the early 1960s to widen the turning.

The Royal Oak Hotel, until its recent closure, was one of the very few hotels left in Sevenoaks. It had been known originally as the Black Bull and was recalled by Victorian diarist, Jane Edwards, as "A large and respectable inn, where balls are held." The hotel also offered well-maintained gardens to the rear.

The Royal Oak Tap was located next to the hotel. It is now a private house.

'My mum worked at the hotel in the 1960s – mostly in the kitchen but she also did some painting and decorating. I used to go with her in the school holidays and earned my first pay packet for helping the chambermaid make up the rooms – 6 old pennies, one for each year of my age. The owners were Mr and Mrs Hitchcock and they lived in the rooms with the corner window, and her mother Mrs Edge lived in the apartment across the garden (I spent a lot of time with her, she always had chocolate). The staff lived in the attic rooms. There were also lots of permanent guests. As a 6-year-old it was a wonderful place, everyone made a lot of fuss of me and the coffee ice cream was so exotic!'

Wendy Crowhurst

'Eileen and Douglas Squibb used to run the pub in the 1960s and maybe early 70's too. When my sisters and I were young my dad used to say to mum on a Sunday lunchtime, "I'm taking the kids out in the pram for some fresh air". Mum was grateful for the peace. Dad was straight down to the Oak Tap. He dropped us kids off in the kitchen where Eileen was preparing their own lunch so he could have a crafty pint or two while Eileen kept an eye on us.'

Vern Gardner

Built in the early eighteenth century and originally a private house, The Coachmaker's Arms stood at 23 High Street and operated for approximately a hundred years, from the early 1850s.

> 'My parents, John and Pauline Walton, lived here from 1966-1988. My folks weren't great at DIY and the layout of the house was very much as the pub must have been – we still had the private bar in the rear lounge and the Gents in the garden! It was also one of the coldest houses I've been in. The cellar was great for my brother's parties, and a popular spot for the boarders of Sevenoaks School'.

Hugh Walton

The Chequers Inn. Once at the heart of market life when cattle pens would have been seen outside the premises. The pub continues to be well used.

The Rock and Fountain stood at 139 London Road and was a well-known venue and cheap lodging house. The site briefly became a car showroom and then a second-hand furniture market before being flattened completely in 2017.

A tavern is believed to have stood on this site since the early 1600s, if not before. Victorian images show a very different structure *(see page 74)*. This photo shows the present premises, now a restaurant, which was rebuilt in 1887 to enable Dorset Street to be widened. The pub was named for the Sackville family, who at one point, were Earls, then Dukes of Dorset.

Local resident Norman Spencer, who lived on South Park, enjoying his pint in the Dorset Arms around 1960.

The tavern looked toward The Vine and War Memorial from its vantage point on Pound Lane. A brewhouse stood here since at least the 1840s and the pub survived until the early 2000s, when it became a restaurant. It closed in 2019.

> 'Spent many a time there as a child and growing up, it was my parents' way of spending time together without us!! They were in the bar, us kids outside or in the side room. Used to like it when the weather was good, and we all spilled onto the grass and played games.'

Sandra Houlden

The Anchor pub photographed in 1961. Most likely dating from the early 18th century, and originally a three-storey building. The pub was remodelled in the early 1920s.

The Bat and Ball public house, which stood at 168 St John's Hill. The Moorcroft family are pictured outside the premises.

The Railway Tavern was located opposite the Bat and Ball pub at the bottom of St John's Hill. Opened in April 1862, it survived until 1978, later having a brief period as Tracks nightclub. At one point a small off-licence, known as the Jug & Bottle, was attached to the side, the entrance to which can be seen on the left in the more modern photo.

> *'I only knew it on a Friday lunch time when some of the Marley Tile factory night shift used it after finishing the 4 night 12 hour shift on Friday morning. Brown paper wage packets, cards, and beer. Would never be allowed today but it seemed fun at the time!'*
>
> **John Gilbert**

'Used to have to sit outside with a packet of crisps and a bottle of Vimto in the 50s. If we were lucky and it was raining, we were allowed in the Jug & Bottle off-licence.'

Alan Crouch

'My brother and I used to take empty bottles back to the Jug & Bottle and get enough 'deposit' money refunded to buy sweets in Manklows on the way home.'

Sarah Putman

The Sennocke Pub, later known as The Farmers, is a much-missed venue and landmark, the loss not helped by the fact that nothing has replaced the building since demolition.

'The Sennocke pub was my childhood home, my parents Alan and Christine Naggs ran it from the early 1970s until the early 1980s! The Brady family ran The Railway & Bicycle pub opposite.'

Jackie Bishenden

'When the Sevenoaks market was at Tubs Hill we used to go in the pub for lunch sometimes. My children loved the market, especially when the animals were there. My dad used to take them there to see the cows, sheep, and pigs etc. In later years, my mum used to work in the newsagents just up from the pub.'

Diane Rose

Charles Draper, landlord of The Halfway House with his wife Bertha nee Welfare, and their children. Bertha Draper was related to the novelist H.G. Wells who wrote The Time Machine while living at Eardley Road. Of their children, Robert, Frank, and Charlie all fought in the First World War. The photo dates from before then, as Charles Draper died in 1903 aged forty-three. A friendly landlord, groundsman at The Vine Cricket Club, as well as a decent player, he received a fulsome obituary in the Sevenoaks Chronicle on 22 May that year.

2

HOTELS

With only one hotel now in the town, it is perhaps hard to imagine how many coaching inns, hotels, and pubs offering rooms for the night, there once were in Sevenoaks. Travellers could rest, eat and drink; horses could do the same. Coaches departed for London from the Royal Oak Hotel, the Amherst Arms in nearby Riverhead, and elsewhere. The Rose and Crown (left) was a popular venue in the heart of the High Street. The sometimes bawdy antics of customers in the cheaper and less reputable public houses were often reported in the Sevenoaks Chronicle. The Royal Crown Hotel was perhaps the most impressive, dominating as it did the top of London Road, with extensive gardens to the rear. Times changed and this once thriving meeting place was demolished in the 1930s.

ROYAL CROWN HOTEL,
LONDON-ROAD, SEVENOAKS.

The Royal Crown Hotel was once at the heart of Sevenoaks Society, hosting banquets, balls, and even auctions. The hotel had extensive gardens and was a popular meeting place. There was also a small farm and vegetable garden that supplied the kitchen. Its last permanent resident, Mrs Mackinnon, was eighty-six when she left her rooms to move to Pembroke Road shortly before its closure. The hotel shut and was pulled down in 1936 and is now the site of The Stag Theatre complex and the Post Office.

Some of the staff of the Royal Crown Hotel pose
for a photograph on the steps of the building.

A hunting crowd gathers outside the Royal Crown Tap, more simply known as the
Crown Tap, adjacent to the hotel.

The Royal Oak Hotel on the corner of Oak Lane was a prominent stopping point for stage and mail coaches to and from London. The hotel provided both meals and accommodation, as did other hotels in town, including the Royal Crown, and the Rose and Crown. Journey time to the capital could take up to four hours.

Close to the centre of town was the Lime Tree Hotel, a temperance hotel which meant that no alcoholic beverages could be served. It was home to a cycling club, had tennis and croquet lawns, and offered a number of leisure activities for guests. It closed in the 1930s and became home to the Sevenoaks News.

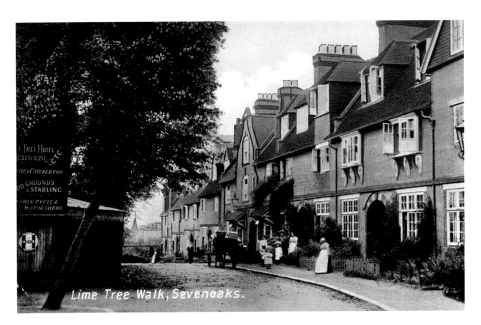

Lime Tree Walk, Sevenoaks.

The Lime Tree Hotel and Lime Tree Walk were designed by the architect Sir Thomas Graham Jackson, whose parents lived locally. Lime Tree Walk was built in a central location in the town for workers. Twenty-four cottages were built with what Jackson himself described as "A simple grace which comes from plain, sensible construction". His aim was to build homes on a beautiful site, from which workmen were able to walk to and from their employment easily, as a move against the trend of working people being forced to move outside of the town to St John's and Bat and Ball.

'My grandfather lived in No. 40, at the bottom, before the church hall was built. He was the first tenant. My father was born there and, later, my brother and myself. Next door, at No. 38, were the three Easterfield sisters: Edith, Eleanor, and Alice. The three houses at the bottom were the only ones with cellars: my grandfather kept his horse there, as it opened into the garden! We moved to No. 26 in 1980 when the council bought the entire road and turned my bedroom at No. 40 into a bathroom! My mother lived in No. 26 almost until she died in 2014. When I grew up, we knew everyone in the road and our doors were never locked!'

Tracey Ball

3

WAR

The War Memorial bears witness to the sacrifices of the servicemen of Sevenoaks in both world wars, but there are other stories too; those of women who nursed, civilians, and the families left behind. The town has also been home to refugees during times of conflict. Belgian accents would have been very familiar from their arrival in 1914, and the town has similarly welcomed Ukrainian refugees just over a century later.

Soldiers, most likely Territorials from the local battalion of The Queen's Own Royal West Kent Regiment, leaving Sevenoaks in the summer of 1914. Crowds followed them as they marched to the station, accompanied by the Town Band and scores of family, friends, and other locals eager to see 'Our Boys' off.

Crowds gather at the station, again during the early days of the Great War. Several contemporary adverts can be seen, including for Whitbread's Ales and Stout, International Stores, F.D. Ibbett, J.S. Charlton and others. Note the smart carriage just to the left too.

Shortly after the outbreak of war in August 1914, Sevenoaks welcomed a significant number of Belgian refugees. Many were soldiers, others were women and children fleeing Belgium after the fall of their country to the Germans. The wounded were cared for in local hospitals of the Voluntary Aid Detachment (V.A.D.), others were found places in family homes. Most returned to Belgium after the war but some married locals and settled here.

The wedding of Emil da Coster and Rosina Caplen. Emil arrived in Sevenoaks as a refugee soldier. He was first listed in the Sevenoaks Chronicle on 23 October 1914 as a patient in the St John's V.A.D. Hospital, where he most likely met Rosina through her work in supporting the local hospitals, and entertaining patients; a natural performer she appeared in many amateur productions. Rosina's father, Frederick (standing right behind his wife Rosina Caplen nee Gunn), was a confectioner, whose business was at 45 High Street. Emil and Rosina married at the Church of St Mary, Kippington, in January 1917.

After the war, Emil was sent to Germany where he drowned accidentally in 1919 while serving with the Belgium Army. His grief-stricken widow crossed Europe in an attempt to have him reburied in his home town of Belsele, St Niklaas, Belgium, or Sevenoaks. Thanks to her efforts he was reburied in the town of his birth and remembered on the Caplen family grave in the churchyard at St Nicholas.

A rare image of a YMCA Hut in Sevenoaks. This hut stood between Hitchen Hatch Lane and Mount Harry Road until it was relocated to The Vine in 1917. The YMCA or Young Men's Christian Association offered servicemen a warm welcome during the Great War. Many men from the north of England were billeted in the town and took advantage of refreshments and entertainments provided by the organisation.

At the end of the war, funds were raised by public subscription for a fitting memorial to the fallen of Sevenoaks. Local people gathered for the unveiling of the war memorial at The Vine in October 1920. The land was donated by Lord Sackville.

The Second World War brought conflict closer to home for the people of Sevenoaks. The photo shows the aftermath of the bombing of Wickenden Road, which killed nine people, including the Webb family who lived at No. 44. Thirteen others were badly injured.

Between August – September 1939, 7,000 children were evacuated to Sevenoaks and the surrounding district. On arrival, children waited to be collected at the cattle market across from the station, with up to ten children in each pen.

Sevenoaks Home Guard was based at Knole Park Golf Club and was commanded by Lieutenant Colonel Shaw MC. By 1st June 1940, the battalion was 1500 strong and divided into nine companies. The Battalion won the Zone Commander's efficiency cup in two consecutive years, beating all other Kent battalions. Pictured top are some of the men on parade in wintry conditions at The Vine, and, below, outside what was then a clinic at the junction of St John's Road and Bradbourne Road. The building is now a children's nursery.

The Home Guard march along the High Street past the International Stores (top) and past Caffyn's garage in the bottom image. It is likely that the photographs were taken during the 'Stand Down' parade at the end of the war. Many of these men were Great War veterans.

Residents of Wickenden and Swaffield Roads, an area that had suffered from bombing during the war, marked VE Day with street parties and other celebrations, as did many other places in and around Sevenoaks.

4

TRANSPORT

Sevenoaks had long been an important stopping point for stage and mail coaches between London and the coast, its many coaching inns a testament to that. The arrival of the railway in Sevenoaks in the 1860s arguably heralded the start of the change from market to commuter town. Before that, would-be rail passengers would need to travel to Tonbridge to catch a London train. Later, Bligh's Bus Station became an important local transport hub, with regular and reliable services throughout the district and beyond.

Sevenoaks station, originally known as Tubs Hill, was built after Bat and Ball Station, which first brought the railway to the town in 1862. What we now regard as the main Sevenoaks station followed six years later in 1868. This image shows station master, Mr Thomas, with some of his staff in the early twentieth century.

The original footbridge was replaced but the station remained largely unchanged until the major refurbishment of the 1970s.

Inside the signal box at Sevenoaks station.

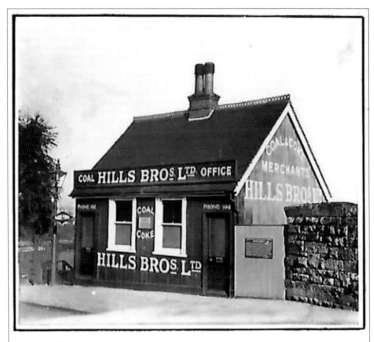

Tubs Hill Station
                    Sevenoaks

An advertisement for Hills Bros. Ltd. a prominent local coal merchant which occupied this little building opposite the station, with coal stored behind it in the yard. It hasn't been occupied for some time but has since had other uses, including a cab office, antiques shop, and as a small yet well-used branch of Richer Sounds.

DRIVER KENDAL
FIREMAN WOOD
S'OAKS   B & B

After 1862, when Bat and Ball station opened, new residents came to live in Sevenoaks. Industries such as brickmaking, quarrying, light engineering, gas works, printing and publishing brought new employees from outside. Building homes for commuters became a major local industry, especially after the second railway opened at Tubs Hill later that decade with faster trains to London – this helped accelerate the growth of the local population.

The ticket office in 1967. After a long decline, the station and its buildings underwent a sympathetic restoration in 2018.

Bligh's Bus Station taken in 1937. 'Under the clock' was a favourite meeting place for many people. Low levels of car ownerhip and a busy and well-staffed bus network meant that it was a well-known place for many locals. After much debate and controversy, the bus station was demolished in 1991 and moved to its current location. It is still remembered fondly, from the cafe, to the illuminated map, and the many memories of meeting here over the decades.

'Meeting place, eating place, date place, hanging out with your mates place, using the loo to put on makeup ready for photos in machine place, and, of course, getting any bus you wanted.'

Ali O'Neil

'Growing up, we never had a car at home, so the bus service was so important to us. I have so many memories as I was in and out of the bus station all the time! The 413 to Chipstead or the 483 and getting off at Bessels Green. Happy days!'

Maggie Dosdale

'The 431 was the only bus from Orpington to Sevenoaks that went via
Halstead, as the 402 went via Badgers Mount. The last evening 431 was
10pm so we always missed the end of any film at Sevenoaks Odeon!'

Wendy Edmeads

'My grandad, Horace Williams, known as "Bert", was a bus driver for thirty-six years in and around the Sevenoaks area. This is him and his bus during that time. He also used to drive the bus route to Windsor. In 1940 he moved into a house in Cramptons Road with his wife, Connie, and their sons, David, Tony, John and Peter.'

Hayley Williams

The 421 in Kemsing on its way toward Sevenoaks, taken in the late 1950s.

'As an eight-year-old, it was a tough walk from Riverhead to Bayham Road School. So at times I could catch the 421 at Bat and Ball to climb St John's Hill. The price of a gobstopper...!'

Chris Chater

A delivery van for the grocery stores of E.J. Payne, parked in Buckhurst Avenue.

Clifton and Ethel Hilder were one of the first owners of a motor car in Sevenoaks. They are pictured in their Benz vehicle next to Ethel's brother Leslie, on a tricycle (right). The Hilders lived at Ashbrook on Vine Court Road.

Norman Spencer *(seen as an older man on page 13)* and brother of Ethel Hilder, with his motorbike at the junction of Vine Court Road and Avenue Road.

5

LEISURE AND CELEBRATIONS

The town offered a range of opportunities for recreation and sporting activities as people took advantage of having more time for leisure, and improved transport links. Photographers have always been on hand to capture events here, some more formal than others. The Vine has become a focal point for many celebrations, from the Coronation of King George V in 1911, to the Platinum Jubilee of his granddaughter, Queen Elizabeth II, in 2022.

There is so much activity in this photo but the eye is drawn to the young man front and centre, holding the camera in a steady gaze. It was taken at a fete to celebrate the Coronation of King George V held on The Vine. Three years later the country would be at war.

Schoolchildren arrive at Knole as part of the Coronation fete in 1911. Patriotic flags held aloft, the banner toward the end of the procession reads 'Council School'. Over three thousand children had marched from The Vine, led by the Town Band.

The town came together less formally to mark the Silver Jubilee of Queen Elizabeth II in 1977.

> *'My dad designed and made that windmill and I have very clear memories of travelling on that float. My brother was given the job of sitting inside the windmill and turning the sails!'*
>
> **Cathy Long**

'This float was by the Sevenoaks Mothers' Club. My mum, Georgina Colbey, was at the front in the white costume and my dad, Alan, was driving.'

Caroline O'Mahony

CORNER OF THE LIME TREE BALLROOM, SEVENOAKS.

The Lime Tree Hotel started life as the Lime Tree Temperance Hotel. The dance hall, seen here, was a popular venue.

An invitation to a dance, possibly to celebrate the engagement of Miss Bowrah and Mr Martin. This card was most likely sent to well-known local shopkeeper Amos Pett *(see page 99)*, and hints at the social activities the middle class of Sevenoaks could enjoy.

Cycling became a fashionable leisure pursuit in the late Victorian period. This photo shows the Lime Tree Cycling Club in 1886, outside the eponymous hotel.

Sevenoaks Football team, here photographed in 1901, was founded in 1883.

Staff gather outside the Odeon Cinema to mark the end of the Second World War. The cinema, first known as the Majestic, was one of four cinemas in the town during this period. The promotional photo for the film 'Casanova Brown' dates from January 1945.

Swimining Baths. Sevenoaks

The swimming baths on Eardley Road opened in 1914. Many of the first patrons were soldiers. Since then, generations of children learnt to swim here.

'Sevenoaks Swimming Club training once a week, followed by oxtail soup from the vending machine, and the school swimming galas!'

Kate Willis

'Loved going there in the 40s and 50s, and cycling home full pelt down Tubs Hill!'

Erica Briton

'We used to live on Eardley Road and my sister and I spent as much time as we could there, learning to swim and dive. I even won a school prize there when I was about 10. I remember the tarpaulin screen, the wire baskets, and the cold changing rooms, along with the Everard family.'

Sandra Houlden

6

KNOLE

Modern visitors come to Knole, like their predecessors, to see the deer and view the great house, which has been in the hands of the National Trust since 1946. Knole avoided the fate of other local stately homes like Montreal and Wildernesse, and remains home to the Sackville-West family. Generations of local residents lived and worked on the estate, some of whom were captured in snapshots, providing a fascinating glimpse of life 'below stairs'.

Tame Deer,   Knole Park, Sevenoaks.

A mix of boys from different social classes getting up close to a deer in Knole Park.

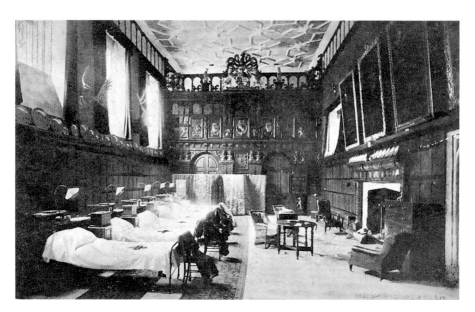

A rare image of the Great Hall at Knole having been converted to a convalescent home for a short time to welcome casualties from the Great War. Lionel 3rd Baron Sackville played a significant part in the war effort, and many of the household staff and estate workers enlisted.

The silent film star, Anna May Wong, who spent some time in Sevenoaks in 1929 whilst recovering from influenza. She was a friend of Eddy Sackville-West, later 5th Baron Sackville. This press photo shows her riding in Knole Park.

Edward Stubbs was Head Gardener for many years, seen here with his wife and children, with some curious objects at their feet.

At the time this photo was taken in September 1929, William Beavin was the oldest employee on the estate. Having been born in 1854, he was seventy-five and still working as a carter.

William Dunmall and his son, Owen, worked on the estate for many years.

Many of these photos were taken by Doris Ivy Pattenden, known as 'Pop'. Doris and her brother John were the children of Thomas Pattenden and his wife Florence, who were employed as wicket (or front hall) porters at the house for many years. Thomas, who was a Territorial soldier, was sent to India following the outbreak of war in 1914, and served there until he died in January 1918. His widow continued in the role for many years, with her children growing up at Knole amid the wider family of servants and estate workers.

> *'For many years, John would remember that when he was little – he was about I suppose 8 or thereabouts, 6 or 8 – walking up and down the Green Court with Lady Sackville, who was knitting scarves for the troops in the trenches. He used to listen to her while she told him stories: fairy stories and adventure stories, and he was always criticised by her for saying "Mmm". So, she used to say 'You must not say Mmmm when I tell you something, you must say "Yes, my Lady". He always remembered that.'*

> **Ian Pattenden**

Thomas Pattenden was one of several staff of Knole who served during the Great War, pictured here in the uniform of The Queen's Own Royal West Kent Regiment.

Harry Record, a friend of Doris Pattenden, photographed feeding a large deer known as 'Billy'.

Florence Pattenden, who continued to work as the wicket porter after the death of her husband. This was unusual, but allowed the family to stay at Knole.

An informal snapshot of Mr Wilfred Booth, butler at Knole, with his children, John and Barbara. His erect bearing perhaps gives away his profession.

The Booth family (Emily Booth was Assistant Housekeeper), with Harry Record, a family friend, on the left. Some staff at Knole took a regular annual holiday together and this snapshot was taken at Winchelsea in 1928.

7

TUBS HILL AND STATION PARADE

Station Parade was once a thriving little community of shops, pubs, and local businesses. Two pubs served weary travellers and commuters, as well as being a watering hole for the many people doing business at the nearby cattle market. Both market and pubs are now gone, and the area is perhaps one of the most changed parts of Sevenoaks. These postcards and photos from an earlier time show the area as it once was.

A gravure style colourised postcard featuring The Sennocke Hotel, later to be renamed The Farmers, opposite Tubs Hill Station. The demolition of this building and the subsequent lack of development has continued to be a source of frustration.

A postcard of Station Parade, which looks Edwardian, or at least pre 1914. The shops remain, but the pubs have disappeared, and the station has been rebuilt completely.

Looking down toward Station Parade. Many of the houses were demolished, and replaced with offices or blocks of flats, and the flow of traffic has increased hugely compared to this early view, when no car can be seen.

A postcard view of St Botolph's Road as it joins Tubs Hill. A familiar scene that has changed little in the intervening years. Next door to the café is a branch of Martins Bank.

French's Dairy at Tubs Hill was one of a number of branches that the business had around town. Dairies were a regular feature of daily life, and either delivered to the home or offered fresh, local produce in store.

Martins Bank had a branch at 2 (later renumbered to 5) St Botolph's Road from 1931. In 1968 a new office was opened at 12 London Road and St Botolph's downgraded to a sub branch. The bank was taken over by Barclays and the branch later moved around the corner to 7 Station Parade. The distinctive grasshopper logo of Martins Bank can be seen hanging outside the branch, which was next door to the Post Office when this photograph was taken in the 1950s.

8

LONDON ROAD

London Road emerges from Tubs Hill as it rises toward the old town. The Royal Crown Hotel once stood at the top, before the road joined with the High Street. Until the early 1900s, much of the land was taken by the impressive operation of Bligh's brewery, from meadow to oast houses. The meadow later became home to the bus station; now replaced by shops and parking. Today, the surviving older buildings contain much of interest, such as the cellars of the old town jail at no's. 14-18. These historic survivors retain the character of this road and sit alongside the newer additions.

A mid-Victorian view of London Road, with the Dorset Arms in the centre unrecognisable from its later incarnation. The pub was transformed for the widening of the street which runs alongside it.

Horse drawn carts dominate in this image of London Road but the smart car outside Youngs signals the changes ahead. Joseph Kay, whose premises stood where Francis Chappell now is, was a bootmaker, as well as collector for the Town Band. He died in 1910 which helps date this photograph to the Edwardian period.

C. Timberlake on the right built and sold 'safety' bicycles, and was located at the entrance to Lime Tree Walk, close to the hotel which served as the base for a cycling club. In recent times, the building has been well known as a branch of Hoads shoe shop, now closed.

A more modern branch of French's dairy from that on Tubs Hill, featured on *page 70*. As the shop sign states, the company had recently taken over the premises from Killick's Dairy.

'Both my parents worked at Youngs. My father, Mac Jones, was the funeral director in the High St store from 1966 until the shop closed and my mum, Phyllis, worked in the ladies' dress department in the 1970s, in the London Road larger shop. The Menswear shop was opposite, on London Road, where the Hardware shop stood until recently.'

Sandra Welham Jones

'Mr Philcox was the display manager, who ruled over us little unworthy window dressers in the long dark tunnel of the basement. Every year we would decorate it to resemble Santa's Lapland hideaway and every year Mr Hobbis, a local pensioner, would weave his way into the cave, bottle of Scotch in hand and surrender himself to the torturous methods of pleasing the unwilling infants that formed a daily crocodile to sit on his lap. Every afternoon we brought him tea and a jam tart. Every year he offered us his manifesto for the next.... "I been comin' here for twenty years. I ain't doing it next year. No I ain't!" I don't think he had many teeth, no matter, it didn't prevent him from imbibing a surreptitious sip of his own hidden refreshment. By 4pm he was generally high as a kite and a lot more tolerant with the kiddies.

One afternoon, bored with the repetition of the season, and preparing his daily snack, we removed the blob of mock cream that always sat in the centre of the jam in his tart. We replaced it with a blob of mock snow..... of which there was no shortage of supply. A thimble-sized lump of pure polystyrene! To be honest, I don't think he noticed the difference. But Philcox enquired as to the reason of our hysteria. Thinking he would get the joke we told him. That was our undoing. For the next month we were banished to working in the freezer.

The freezer was the last window on the right as you look at the store. It was an independent showcase with not a smidgen of heat. It was the last post. A glass coffin where the public could view one's dying motions. Then suddenly that was Christmas, all over and we were packing up the twinkly lights, sweeping away the mock snow, putting the reindeer back in their boxes, and Santa metamorphosed back into a sozzled Mr Hobbis again. "Well Cheerio chaps..... see you all next year!"'

Miv Watts

Joe Russell was a popular and long-serving barber, well known in the town. Joe is seen here at the start of his career, outside the front of barber's shop P.J. French, which stood next to Gower and Whites on Dorset Street. Joe later had his own premises on the street, which many will remember.

'When I was a young kid my dad used to take me to Joe's for a haircut. I remember Joe would be smoking a roll-up whilst cutting my hair and the ash would get longer and longer. I would momentarily look away and when I looked back in the mirror I discovered the ash had disappeared, then a generous dollop of Brylcreem would be applied on my head whether I wanted it or not, I am sure it was to cover up the ash.'

Vern Gardner

Charles Essenhigh Corke was arguably the leading local photographer of his day. He was followed into the business by his talented son, Henry, who died young in 1919, aged thirty-five. Their studios occupied a prominent place in the town at 39 and 43 London Road. Examples of their work and that of other local studios can regularly be found for sale. During the First World War, they offered a free photograph to those serving and many took the opportunity, whether local men in uniform, nurses, or men from the north of England who were billeted in Sevenoaks.

In this picture the building most recently known as the Hardware Store was occupied by A. Baker, a confectioner and tobacconist. The shop remained in the hands of the Baker family until the 1960s. Next to him was William Percy Vallins, a florist and fruiterer. The Essenhigh Corke studio stood opposite these businesses and can be seen on the right.

A fine image of Henry Ellman's grocery store which occupied a prime position on London Road from 1881. On retirement he handed over the business to his former manager, Mr Stevens, and it later became well-known as Uridges. In more recent times it was known as Window Scene, which sold fabrics and soft furnishings, and also incorporated a restaurant.

Two postcard views which label the same stretch of road, both Tubs Hill and London
Road. These shops and houses that once overlooked Bligh's meadow and hop gardens
now face the Marks and Spencer shop and car park.

Bank Cottages seen from The Drive in the early 1900s before the righthand row were demolished to make way for construction of the Emily Jackson Hospital, designed by her brother, architect Sir Thomas Graham Jackson. St Luke's church is just visible to the left, behind the lefthand row of cottages.

9

UPPER HIGH STREET

With London Road and the High Street having merged, the road curves round past Raley's Corner, and heads on south, with commanding views over The Weald. A church has stood on the site of St Nicholas for a thousand years, first being recorded in the Textus Roffensis (compiled c1120). Today the area has a mix of uses, and continues to be home for some. The picturesque Six Bells Lane being one example.

A mid-Victorian photograph of the Upper High Street at Raley's Corner. At the centre of the image on the lefthand side is Stanger & Co., one of the early photographers who had premises in the town. The weather and traffic have caused the muddy conditions in the road.

A later view of Raley's Corner looking in the other direction, and taken between the wars, with W.J. Warren and The Little Boot Shop, which was at that address between 1924 and 1932. The buildings 31-37 on the left were originally a single property.

Two restaurants faced each other in this part of the town. The Top O' the Hill on the left, and French restaurant, Le Chantecler, on the right.

The White House stood opposite The Red House at the top of Sevenoaks High Street. Originally two cottages, the grand Georgian front had been added in 1810. Since the 1920s it had been home to an antiques business.

Despite being listed, and a strong public campaign to save it in the early 1960s, an inquiry found that it was riddled with deathwatch beetle and dry rot, and the building was demolished, robbing the town of a grand structure many thought worthy of preservation.

Two Victorian views looking north and south from the Upper High Street. At this time the road surface consisted of compacted dirt and stone, rather than tarmac. The opposing views also show the class divisions in local society, from the road sweeper to the gentleman in the top hat.

The rear of 33-37 High Street on the corner with Six Bells Lane with its nine dormer windows. A quintessentially English look at the top of the town. The lean of the chimneys is a defect known as sulphate attack, which causes them to lean into the prevailing weather.

Two views of Six Bells Lane taken in 1931. The picturesque cobbled lane derives its name from the original six bells of nearby St Nicholas church.

The memorial cross for the fallen of the Great War outside St Nicholas Church. Designed by Sir Thomas Graham Jackson, who was responsible for Lime Tree Walk, only the base now stands in the original position.

The churchyard extension at St Nicholas. Postcards like this may seem odd to us today but they could serve as a memento to loved ones, especially those unable to attend a funeral. The churchyard extension is the last resting place of some notable former residents and includes two daughters of Charles Dickens. Former rector, Reverend John Rooker, is buried here with his wife, Adele, as are some casualties of the Great War. The more accessible earlier churchyard is home to the tomb of Francis Austen, once of The Red House (now the home of Knocker & Foskett), and great uncle of the novelist Jane Austen.

The Reverend John Rooker and his wife, Adele nee Thompson. As Rector, Rooker was a significant figure in town life. His privately published 'Memoir of the Great War for Children' is a valuable insight into life at the time.

A view of the east end of the church, taken in 1870, showing the box pews that were removed only a few years later at the end of the decade. Open pews were then installed, the wood being sourced from Knole.

A view of the west end of the church.

In the early 1990s, a significant excavation took place. Controversial at the time, over five hundred burials, some dating from the 11th century were removed, creating space for an expansion of the church buildings and creation of the undercroft.

10

HIGH STREET

Sevenoaks was shaped by two roads, originally medieval drove roads, along which animals were taken from the North Downs to the weald. These routes, which we know now as London Road and the High Street, came together at the top of the town and led on south. The town's location made it a natural stopping point on the coach routes to and from the capital. Hotels and pubs, Bligh's and Smiths' breweries, department stores, and residential houses, as well as the historic market, long characterised the High Street, which now serves the needs of a population very different to that of the original market town.

A late-Victorian image of the junction of London Road and the High Street, showing the Sevenoaks Coffee Tavern, which was open from 1886 until 1901. The building was demolished in 1925 and replaced by the single storey edifice we are familiar with today.

A mid-Victorian view, looking north from the top of the High Street with a wide expanse where the old market would be held. At one time the building on the left was part bank, part private residence (for the Salmon family, among others), part printing press, and part shop.

Two opposing views of the High Street, looking north and south. Taken during the mid-Victorian period, the photographer would have required every person to stand still long enough to capture the image without blurring. The children outside the Rose and Crown Hotel being especially well behaved.

A charabanc (early motor coach) parked outside the offices of the Sevenoaks Chronicle and the Kent and Sussex Courier. The chemist, Pain & Powell, can be seen next door.

A little further down the High Street than the previous photo, children stare at the smart car, parked outside a branch of Boots, Warren's, and Lloyds Bank.

Amos Pett, a prominent resident and businessman, photographed outside his basket shop on the High Street. It was Amos Pett who received the invitation to the dance at the Lime Tree Hotel on *page 52.*

Family grocers, R.A.Stiles, operated at 78 High Street, from the early 1890s until 1914, on what is now the site of Lorimers. The building was finally demolished in 1984.

A busy and festive view of the High Street with Father Christmas driving through the town. Several once well-known shops can be seen in this image. Gower & White were popular butchers, while on the opposite side, the Parris bakery did a brisk trade. Father Christmas and his gifts were destined for the Children's Hospital, having been donated by the Odeon cinema.

The staff of Sevenoaks Woolworths, taken at the rear of the premises in 1950. Woolworths remained a much-loved shop until its closure.

The South Suburban Co-operative Society opened on the High Street in 1930. The shop had several departments, selling everything from groceries to drapery and footwear. It was refurbished as a supermarket in the 1970s.

'This is my mum when she was manageress of Sevenoaks Co Op Drapery Department by the old Bus Station. It must have been about 1950/51 as she was holding the bolt of material up to hide the bump that was to become me in July 1951! Her name was Elsie Young and we lived above Owen Harrison Antiques on London Road. I remember her telling me that there were often car accidents in the narrow road that led up to the Bus Station and when she heard the squeal of brakes and tyres followed by the crash she used to faint, and the sales assistants used to lay her on the counter to recover!'

Diana Gibb

The High Street looking south with Marsh & Whytnie drapers on the right. On the immediate left is Simmonds, which helps date the photo to before 1936. Further along, the Holmesdale Pub can be seen on the left.

The Electricity Co., Walkers Stores, and Edmund Goodrich on the left hand side of the High Street.

High Street, Sevenoaks

The junction of the High Street and Pembroke Road. The Electric Cinema (on the left of the photograph) first opened in 1910 on the site of the old Smith's brewery. It was owned by Frank Robinson, proprietor of the Royal Oak Hotel and a local councillor, who saw the potential in moving pictures. The cinema was remodelled in 1926 and completely rebuilt in 1935 when it was officially opened that November by Lord Sackville.

Following Frank Robinson's death in 1929, the cinema remained in the hands of his family, with his son Richard taking over. The cinema eventually became the Plaza and then the Granada. The building was ultimately demolished as part of the works to create Suffolk Way.

The former Bethlehem farmhouse (seen on the left) was leased by Samuel Bligh, father of John, in 1852 and would become known as Bligh's Hotel. The farm, and John Bligh's Holmesdale brewery (rebuilt in 1882), with oasthouses, hop gardens, and meadow, were a significant part of the town, together with Smith's brewery opposite (its distinctive chimney can be seen in the distance on the right). The barn (below) and oast houses were demolished just a few years after the Great War, but the original timber-framed building still survives as a public house.

The old oast houses (above) as they faced on to Pembroke Road, taken in 1919. Here, in the heart of town, hops were grown and beer brewed to be sold locally, primarily in the twenty-seven public houses John Bligh owned. The aromas produced by the brewing process would have been familiar to residents, whether teetotal or not.

A rare view of Bligh's farmhouse taken across the meadow from Pembroke Road. The meadow became the site of the old bus station in 1936, before being redeveloped in the 1990s into the shops and car park we are familiar with today.

II

KIPPINGTON

Kippington House and estate once covered two hundred and sixty eight acres. Owners of the house included the Austen family, who later sold to William Thompson, a local benefactor, responsible for the building of St Mary's church. Kippington is still home to some grand houses, others like Bulimba and Gavrock have been demolished, and the area has seen steady development.

St. Mary's, Kippington.

(Copyright.)

The Church of St Mary, Kippington. Financed by William Thompson, a wealthy tea merchant, the church was consecrated in 1880. Thompson had served as a church warden at St Nicholas church, but established St Mary's to ensure that his more evangelical beliefs were met. His son, Henry Percy Thompson, served as vicar from 1895-1919.

Kippington Meadow was gifted to the town in 1908 by Reverend Henry Thompson, on the understanding that there would be no development. It remains a well-used and tranquil area.

'Our driveway in Oakhill Road was opposite Kippington Meadow so it was a fabulous place to play. Loved it when the grass was cut as it was left for us to turn into dens. Happy memories of the late 1950s and '60s'.

Carolyn Ireland

A scene at Beechmont House taken in the 1860s during a croquet match. The stiff and formal nature of the poses demonstrate how everyone would have been told to stay still for long enough for the photographer to capture the image.

During the Second World War, the house, which had been requisitioned by the Army to billet women serving with the ATS, was hit by a bomb. While most of the women had already arrived in Knole Park for work that morning, two of their number, Violet Gertrude Calderwood and Grace Mary Potter, were killed on 14 July 1944. Both women are buried at Greatness Cemetery, the only two female casualties of that war to be buried in Sevenoaks.

A grand house set in about twenty acres adjacent to St Mary's Church, Bulimba was built in in 1890/1 by William Hemmant, a British-Australian politician who served in the Legislative Assembly of Queensland from 1871 to 1876, and the house took its name from a suburb of Brisbane. It was demolished in 1933.

12

THE VINE

The Vine is best known as home to one of the oldest cricket grounds in the world. The earliest recorded match played there was held in September 1734. The ground was later given to the town in 1773 by John Frederick Sackville, 3rd Duke of Dorset, himself a keen cricketer. After the Great War, adjacent land known as The Vine Waste, was donated by the then Lord Sackville as a home for the town's War Memorial. These two features dominate the area. Although now surrounded by housing, The Vine remains a focal point for sport and recreation.

The Constitutional Club was built in 1889. Also known as the Conservative Club, it closed in 1957 and was converted into apartments in the 1990s. The Club Hall that stood at the rear of the building was destroyed by a bomb in 1940.

Cattle being led from the town in the direction of St Botolph's Road, when livestock was still a common sight in the heart of Sevenoaks. The rear of the Club Hall, which stood behind the Constitutional Club can also be seen in this image.

Crowds gather to hear Winston Churchill speak in favour of local Conservative candidate, (later Sir) John Rodgers, during the General Election campaign of 1950. The great man himself can be seen at the window of the Constitutional Club. An estimated crowd of two thousand turned out to see him. Sir John represented Sevenoaks in Parliament from 1950 until 1979.

A view of The Vine between the wars, with Turner's Nursery on the left.

The firm of J.H. Lorimer, now familiar to us only from its premises on the High Street, once also ran The Vine Post Office. Their premises are seen on the right in this image, with a staff member adopting a nonchalant pose. This little row of shops served the needs of residents living near The Vine.

Looking north along the Dartford Road, with the Vine Baptist Church on Park Lane to the right.

An interesting view of St Botolphs Road, which was built in 1877. However, it was not until twenty years later when the St Botolph estate was sold, that house building began in earnest and two other roads, The Drive, and Pembroke Road, were created.

Dartford Road looking toward St John's. A view that has changed little over the years, although some of the large private houses, such as Egdean, were demolished to make way for smaller houses in their place. The postcard shows the long fences that bordered these properties.

Avenue House School styled itself as 'The High School for Boys' and opened in 1886. The 1891 census shows there were then twenty-five pupils aged from 9 to 15.

The school stood on Avenue Road between Dartford Road and Vine Court Road. It was demolished in 1934 and has been replaced by a more modern home.

Walthamstow Hall, Sevenoaks

Walthamstow Hall School, known locally as 'Wally Hall', was founded in 1838 in Walthamstow. The school moved to Sevenoaks in 1882 and at the time was the largest and most expensive building in the town. It had been founded by Martha Foulger 'to provide for the daughters of Christian missionaries a thoroughly good and liberal education'.

'I was there from 1969 until 1974. Miss Blackburn was headmistress in my first year, followed by the formidable Miss Davies. Happy days!'

Kim Spackman

13

ST JOHN'S

St John's lies to the north, outside of the original town. It was here that the notorious town workhouse was located before being nationally condemned in the early 1840s. It was here too, amidst the fields and orchards, and Wickenden Woods, that saw the growth of housing, shops and other amenities, after the arrival of the railway in Bat and Ball. The development of the St John's area, as well as neighbouring Greatness, and Hartslands, brought new homes for the working classes, schools, and public houses. It continues to be a vibrant area, now joined to the town, but still with its own identity.

The church at the top of St John's Hill, now the United Reform Church. The 130 ft tall spire was removed on safety grounds in 1880.

The top of Mount Harry Road as it joins Dartford Road. The road has seen much recent development, with some properties demolished and replaced by flats or new houses, but it still retains a sense of its past as a grand thoroughfare, home to the middle class of Sevenoaks, developed after the railway arrived at Tubs Hill.

Two fine images by local photographer Ernest Fielder, of Barrack Corner at the top of St John's Hill. To the right, The Greyhound Inn is visible next to the old public conveniences, and to the far right of the image, the garden wall of 'The Limes' that once stood between the shops can be seen.

Blinds pulled down on a warm summer day with just three small children caught by the photographer.

George Kipps, a butcher with premises on Dartford Terrace at the top of St John's Hill near the junction with Mount Harry Road, pictured outside his shop with an impressive display of produce. The Sevenoaks Chronicle once noted that "He has a natural aptitude for such exhibitions, and as before nothing is wanting in detail to make his premises and supplies as attractive as possible. First-class quality is evidently with him the cardinal point, and the forethought shown in the selection of cattle, sheep, pigs, poultry, etc. places him in the first rank of public caterers."

George Harry Mullen pictured outside his shop at 6, St John's Hill, with daughter Violet, and staff, one of whom is holding a black cat. Mr Mullen took over the shop from his employer Frank Rowley in 1922, and worked for the business for a total of fifty-six years.

Upper St. John's, Sevenoaks

This row of shops has remained largely unchanged over the years, although the canopies seen in this postcard are no longer necessary.

Blow's grocery shop was founded in 1891 by Joseph Blow, who was succeeded by his daughter, who ran the shop until her retirement in 1984. The shop window display celebrates the Coronation of King George VI, which dates the photo to May 1937.

Miss Blow pictured in the shop started by her father.

A more recent photograph of these shops with G.W. Medhurst & Son, now the butcher of choice, and a fleet of delivery vans parked outside the premises.

The bakery on the corner of Dartford Terrace was run by Herbert Hill. One of his sons, John Newton Hill, served with the Imperial Camel Corps during the Great War. His daughter, Netta Muskett, became a well-known romantic novelist and co-founder of the Romantic Novelist Association.

This photograph was taken in June 1946 when these premises were offered for sale. The shop on the left is 8 Upper St John's Hill, occupied by Mr. J. B. Plenty a Newsagent, Fancy Goods Dealer, Bookseller and Tobacconist. Next door is No 6, occupied by Mr. G. H. Mullen, who was a High Class Grocer, Provision, Wine and Spirit Merchant.

'During the 1970s and 80s the newsagents was owned and run by my late husband, Fred Lane (in the photo) and myself. We lived in the flat above the shop and loved our years there and our customers. On the right is Threshers the Wine Merchant whose manager was Ron Gold. To the left of the photo is the Greyhound Pub.'

Lynn Lane

Fred Lane behind the counter in his shop.

Cubs and scouts heading off to camp, taken on Hollybush Lane in August 1943.
Douglas Richter, whose family were longstanding Sevenoaks residents is in the group.
He is also seen in the photograph below pushing his friend in a homemade cart made
from an old Sunlight soap box.

Mr Peacock outside his shop, Hearn and Peacock, on Hollybush Lane. The shop
was popular with pupils from the nearby Cobden Road School.

> *'This is my grandad. The shop was on Hollybush Lane. My dad was born in*
> *the three bedroom flat above the shop. Dad was born in 1936 and was one*
> *of seven boys who lived in there. Grandad was in the Home Guard during*
> *the war, and regularly patrolled the local area at night, and often ended up*
> *in the Camden Arms.'*

Stuart Peacock

Children line up in the Cobden Road School playground in this photo taken in 1923.

Cobden Road, which, apart from the noticeable lack of cars vying for a parking space, remains largely unchanged. The road has the sad honour of being home to the largest number of men from any street in Sevenoaks to have died in the Great War. Many of these men would have attended Cobden Road School at the top of the road, where there is now a memorial plaque to them.

The Quakers Hall Bakery, which was located at corner of Cobden Road and Quakers Hall Lane. Freshly baked loaves, ready for delivery, can be seen in the cart. The site had a number of different uses over the years and has now been demolished and replaced by apartments.

Quaker's Hall Lane with the turning to Bushes Road (now Prospect Road) on the right. St John's National School on the right has been replaced by a modern block of flats.

'Those railings around the school had very sharp points on them which were cut off in 1962, to the sorrow of Mr Godden the Head Teacher who remarked that people who tried to climb over the fence and became impaled were unlikely to do it again. Different times!'

Tim Sanderson

St John's church was built in the late 1850s, in response to the population growth of the town, particularly of the St John's area. The front gateway in this image has now been closed and the ivy cleared away, but the church still thrives and serves the community.

St John's Hill looking north from the junction with Quakers Hall Lane.

Bradbourne College stood at the junction of Bayham Road and Quakers Hall Lane. A High School for 'Girls of the private and professional classes', it also offered a boys preparatory school and a 'Thorough education and happy home life'. The building survives and has been divided into apartments.

Hartslands Road taken by Ernest Fielder. The Hartslands area was originally fourteen acres of fields that were purchased by builder and developer Daniel Grover in the late 1830s. The area became a working-class 'village' with its own shops, schools, pubs, and places of worship.

In the interwar period, housing gradually came to replace once open fields and nurseries that lined St John's Hill. The houses here were built in 1934.

An illustration from an advert for new homes on Wickenden Road. Built on the site of a former garden nursery, the houses were described as 'compact, well built, semi-detached houses. The best value ever offered.'

> '*My grandmother and grandfather lived at 32 Wickenden, and my aunt and uncle lived at No. 77. One of my earliest memories was going to my grandfather's house after a V2 landed just down the road; houses were flattened and my grandfather's house had all the windows blown out and ceilings collapsed.*'

Alan Crouch

The New Inn stood at 75 St John's Hill until it closed in 2014. Don's shoe shop occupied the smaller space on the right. The pub was demolished and replaced by modern flats.

Some buildings on St John's Hill were knocked down to make way for new. These cottages on the corner of Wickenden Road and St John's Hill were demolished in 1946.

An interesting photo of St John's Hill, showing the nursery of R.A. Neal Ltd. on the right before it was used for housing. In the distance is the former nurses' home, while on the left is the tobacconist and sweet shop, with the New Picture Theatre, which became the Carlton cinema, just a little further on. At the time this was taken, the tobacconist is run by T.H. Terry but it was later taken over by Mr. and Mrs. Tidy, pictured below.

'I remember my dad popping into Tidy's for his rolling tobacco. I remember it was very small but there were lots of jars of sweets.'

Nicki Murphy

A nice image of the bottom of St John's Hill around the early 1930s. Ernest Fielder, the photographer who took many photos in and around St John's and elsewhere, had premises at the top of this parade of shops on the right at No. 121. Martins stores is to the right of his at No.125.

'I remember Woolett & Sharp motorcycles. Martins had stores on both sides of the road, and I went to St John's Primary School with their daughter. Just down from the motorcycle shop was a bakers. The bakers and the fishmongers were run by my grandparents.'

Kevin Sweet

'I bought my first camera from Fielders, a little box with two flickup squares as a viewfinder with no glass in them! Many of my teenage photos were taken with it. At that time I lived in St. Johns Road and went to Walthamstow Hall School. In the 1950s there was a forge near the crossroads where I watched horses being shod.'

Erica Britton

'The first shop was Seaker Butcher's, my grandfather and father owned it. They also had a shop at the crossroads in Borough Green. Next door to them became Susan's, a second-hand shop. Then there was a chemist, a bookmakers, and the last shop was Romas hardware.'

Tracey Stanton-Salter

A view of lower St John's Hill showing the Castle Inn at No. 87. The pub closed in 2015. The shopfronts are still recognisable today.

Although these shops have changed hands many times on this road, particularly on the right-hand side, it remains familiar.

St. John's Hill, Sevenoaks.

A good view of the bottom of St John's Hill. The shop sign on the left says W. J. Hammerton. William Joseph Hammerton had been born within the sound of Bow Bells, making him a genuine Cockney. He took over the premises from a Mr Randall and ran a combined hairdressers and newsagents before the business was taken over by his son. Judging by the cars, this doesn't seem later than early 1930s.

THE HOSPITAL, SEVENOAKS.

The Sevenoaks and Holmesdale Cottage Hospital opened in 1873 after a campaign to raise funds to purchase the land and finance building works. With several new additions, the hospital still thrives today. This postcard dates from the early 1900s.

Hillingdon Avenue, with Sevenoaks Hospital visible on the left.

'I lived in Hillingdon Avenue at the Wildernesse Mount end from the early 1970s till I left home. Despite being such a long road, you still used to know many people that lived there. Fond memories.'

Caroline O'Mahony

A view of Greatness and the mill pond dating from the early 1930s, judging by the car in the foreground. ARC Motors (owned by A R Chatfield) can be seen in the centre rear. The pond is one of the last remaining links to the silk and flour mills once owned by the Nouailles family.

14

RIVERHEAD

Once a small village, Riverhead was a rural community bordered by Montreal and Bradbourne Parks, and nearby Chipstead Place. Many residents would have worked for these estates, which were significant local employers. The village remained largely unchanged until a programme of demolition and road widening took place in the 1960s.

Despite these physical changes, it retains much of value, including its historic inns, the former Amherst Arms, and the Bullfinch. St Mary's Riverhead was built in 1831. The churchyard is the last resting place of Bridget Aurea Lambarde, a nurse during the Great War, who died in the influenza pandemic in 1919, and of the Webb family of Wickenden Road, killed toward the end of the Second World War in March 1945.

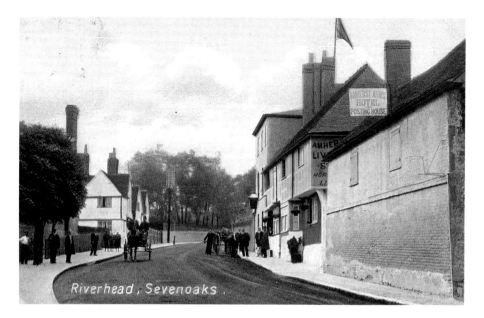

The Amherst Arms and Hotel which took its name from the Amherst earldom, stood on the edge of the Montreal Estate. Parts of the building date from the 16th century. Although still a recognisable view, some development has replaced the land and trees seen here as the road inclines toward Tubs Hill. The gardens at the rear evoke a gentler age.

An aerial view of the Amherst Arms taken from the tower of St Mary's, Riverhead, once again emphasising the rural nature of the area until relatively recently.

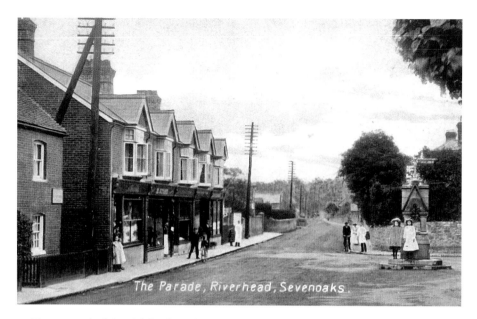

The Parade, Riverhead, Sevenoaks.

The removal of the old drinking fountain, seen in this postcard, which had stood in the same position since Queen Victoria's Diamond Jubilee in 1897, caused much uproar amongst local people. For many years, fountains such as these, were one of the few sources of clean drinking water.

The well-known parade of shops at the bottom of Worships Hill and Chipstead Lane. Father and son, both named Richard Shorey, ran the butchers on the left from around 1870 until the early 1900s when it was taken over by Mr Rogers *(see page 148)*. Richard Shorey junior emigrated to Australia after having sold the family business.

The Riverhead branch of F. Pearce & Sons, a fishmonger who had another branch in Sevenoaks, originally on Dorset Street and then at 94 High Street. This branch was managed by Harry Riley, Fred Pearce's son-in-law and it is most likely him in the doorway with his children Fred, Nellie, Charlie, and Annie, plus a member of staff, and the delivery boy posing with his bicycle.

Frank Rogers outside his shop in Riverhead, with his only son, Ronald.

'Frank Rogers was my great grandfather who was originally a master butcher and subsequently developed and owned Homestead Farm in Rye Lane, Otford (sold by my grandparents in 1971). He and other family members are buried at Greatness Cemetery. Frank is shown in this photo with his son, Ronald, who was killed in a road accident the day before his sixth birthday. The inquest and circumstance of his death were reported widely.'

Steve McCombe

London Rd., Riverhead.

The Bullfinch has long been a local landmark and is an important survivor in the area.

'This pub was the place to be, always packed to the rafters. It had a much lower beamed ceiling then, changed after Pepe the landlord left, and more so after the extensions and refurbishment to its present size. Due to its location, it always attracted a lot of people from Orpington and Bromley.'

Grant Burgess

'Late 70s, early 80s, if you couldn't find who you were looking for in The Bullfinch, they'd be in The Chequers, except when the first night Quadrophenia was shown in The Stag/Odeon, as Royston Edwards and quite a few other local people were in that film.'

Nigel King

Bradbourne Hall, around the time that it was purchased by Francis Crawshay in 1867. A well-known eccentric who had moved from Wales, he refurbished the Hall and developed the gardens, as well as erecting a Druidic stone circle within the grounds, some of which now survives in private gardens. The second image shows Francis standing in the grounds when the garden was being landscaped. In the first photo, two cannon, a fountain, and the locally famous 'Bradbourne bell' can be seen. The building with the three box gabled roofs in the background (top) is what became the ambulance station in later years, after the roof had been replaced. The Hall was later owned by the Lambarde family until they sold it in the 1920s. It was finally demolished in 1936 and Nos. 10-18 Robyns Way now stand on the site.

Montreal, Sevenoaks.

Montreal House, built in the mid-eighteenth century on the site of Brooks Place, an earlier Tudor property, became the seat of the Earls Amherst. The large estate and family home was a significant employer of local people. The last Earl Amherst, a friend of Noel Coward, died in 1993. The estate has been much divided and built upon. The house was demolished in 1936 and little of significance remains.

15

SEAL

Many of the residents of Seal worked on the local estates and farms. Some were employed at Wildernesse and Knole. Most of the village pubs have disappeared and the area is now popular with commuters, rather than estate workers. Wildernesse House was eventually sold by the Hillingdon family, and had a number of guises before it became a school for the blind, and latterly, redesigned for retirement living.

An instantly recognisable view of Seal Village, captured in a postcard dated 1905. The shop on the corner of Park Lane was once a hardware store.

The village High Street in the 1930s.

The High Street with the Forge garage on the left, and The Crown Inn opposite.

A view of Seal from a different direction. Many of the local postcards focus on the view from The Crown Inn looking up the hill. Here you can see the sign for The Copper Kettle in the foreground. Opposite is Swifts garage.

'If a journey was near or far, you knew you were nearly home when you got to the Copper Kettle!'

Richard Platts

A view of the High Street showing the Kentish Yeoman on the right. The building dates from at least the fifteenth century, its later façade concealing a Kentish Hall House. The venue also offered gardens at the rear (pictured below).

Bassett's Garage on Seal High Street provided a range of services, from selling petrol, and car maintenance, to repairing boots and selling radios. The garage was taken over by Bob Bates in 1933.

The church of St Peter and St Paul, in Seal. There are five graves in the care of the Commonwealth War Graves Commission in the churchyard, including that of Hon. Geoffrey Edward Mills, son of the 1st Lord Hillingdon, who died in 1917 whilst serving as a commander with the Royal Naval Volunteer Reserve. A number of former Knole Estate workers are also buried here, including Edward Stubbs, a former head gardener *(see page 60)*.

Wildernesse Drive, Seal

The impressive avenue of 'Waterloo Limes' with its trees planted in honour of the
visit to Wildernesse House by the Duke of Wellington in 1815, just a few months
before his victory over Napoleon. Wellington visited the house again in 1832.

The Wildernesse, Seal. Kent.   34.

Wildernesse House, part of the sprawling Wildernesse estate, that once covered five hundred acres, was owned by the Marquess of Camden during the 19th century before he leased, and then sold it, to Charles Henry Mills, 1st Lord Hillingdon, in whose family it remained until the 1920s. The family extended the house and introduced gas, mains water, and electricity.

The stables became home to a hospital of the Voluntary Aid Detachment during the Great War. Lord Hillingdon's daughter, Hon. Violet Mills, was honoured by the King for her work at the hospital. The house was later purchased by the Royal London School for the Blind and renamed Dorton House.

The Hall, Wildernesse, Seal. Kent.   30.

In recent years, the house has been refurbished and converted into high-end retirement apartments, while still retaining its character and many original features. The latter two photographs of the interior were taken in July 1889.

IMAGE CREDITS

Unless otherwise stated, images are in the private collection of the author, or others who wish to remain anonymous. I am grateful to the photographers, and postcard publishers for the rich legacy they have left for the historian.

My thanks to Sevenoaks Library for permission to reproduce images from their collection. Any omissions are unintentional.

Page 8 bottom (Sarah Rapley), page 13 second image and page 47 (Alec Stevenson), page 15 Anchor Pub Creative Commons Licence CC BY-SA 3.0 DEED; page 18 Jackie Bishenden; page 19 Fiona Draper; page 30 Ann Pieters; page 31 Cadbury Research Library: Special Collections, University of Birmingham (YMCA archive, ref: YMCA/4/1/1/Q/135); page 35 Mary Ann Ellis; page 39 Roger Sheldon; pages 41 & 42 Bat and Ball station; page 45 Hayley Williams; page 51 (bottom) Caroline Mahony; page 60 top Julia Neville; pages 60 (bottom) to 65 the Pattenden family; page 71 Martins Bank Image © Martins Bank Archive Collections; page 76 Diana Gibb; page 77 the Russell family; page 79, Ellman's stores by permission of Dr Anthony J R Pawley; page 81 Tim Pearce (and page 105 (bottom); page 93 Ian Walker; page 100 (Woolworths) Julia Griffith; pages 123, 134 (bottom), 137 (top), by permission of the family of the late Ernest Fielder; page 128 Lynn Lane; pages 129 and 136 page Sally Sharp; page 137 (bottom) Jo Marshall; page 148 Steve McCombe; page 150 Roger Sheldon; page 157 (top) the Bassett family; various from the private collections of Keith Wade, and Brian Eveleigh. Author photograph by Sebastian Stead photography

© Kent County Council Sevenoaks Library (Anckorn Collection) images on pages 13 (top); 20; 24 (top); 32 & 33; 39; 74 (top);78; 86; 88; 92; 94; 97; 104 (bottom); 105 (top); 132 (top); 135.

And from the library archive: pages 14, 101, 145. Pages 53 (bottom), 125 (bottom), and 126 © Kent County Council Sevenoaks Museum

Pages 84 (top), 96 (bottom), 104 (top), 110, 111, 160 (bottom), and 161. Source: Historic England Archive

BIBLIOGRAPHY

Gordon Anckorn (1979), A Sevenoaks Camera (Ashgrove Press: Sevenoaks)

Gordon Anckorn ((1984), Sevenoaks Memories (Ashgrove Press: Sevenoaks)

Philip Burgess (2001) Then and Now Sevenoaks (Tempus Publishing Limited)

John Dunlop (1964), The Pleasant Town of Sevenoaks (Caxton and Holmesdale Press: Sevenoaks)

Jean Fox et al (2007), Seal, the Story of a Parish (Phillimore & Co. Hampshire)

K. R. Gulvin (1980) Kent Home Guard, A History (Tonbridge Printers Ltd.)

David Killingray & Elizabeth Purves (2012), Sevenoaks, An historical dictionary (Phillimore & Co. Hampshire)

David Killingray and Iain Taylor (2022), Sevenoaks 1790-1914, Risk and Choice in West Kent (UH Press)

Bob Ogley & Roger Perkins (1999), Sevenoaks Chronicle of the Century (Froglets Publications: Westerham)

Elizabeth Purves, Geraldine Tucker, Keith Wade (2019) Sevenoaks, A Remarkable Town (Silver Pines Press)

Christopher Rayner (1997), Sevenoaks Past (Phillimore & Co. Ltd.)

Reverend John Rooker, A History of the War for Children (privately published)

Robert Sackville West ((2010), Inheritance, The Story of Knole and the Sackvilles (Bloomsbury)

Vita Sackville-West (1937), Pepita (Hogarth Press: London)

Ed Thompson & Philip Clucas (2013) Sevenoaks St. John's – the Past in Pictures (Hopgarden Press)

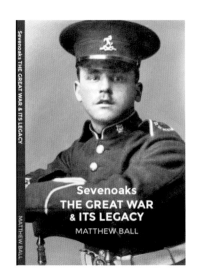

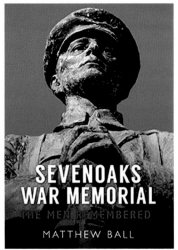

ABOUT THE AUTHOR

Matthew Ball is an historian and genealogist based in Sevenoaks, Kent.

Since 2013 Matthew has run an award-winning community history project on Sevenoaks in the Great War and now also runs a blog and publishes research on The Queen's Own Royal West Kent Regiment during the conflict. He also runs Sevenoaks History Hub on Facebook

Matthew is passionate about local history and genealogy and has conducted research throughout the UK and abroad. He has also published two books on Sevenoaks during the Great War and is currently researching his next book.

In 2022 Matthew was elected an Associate Fellow of The Royal Historical Society.

Read more at
Matthew-Ball.uk

Authentic
Reconstruction